W9-CLB-974

What We Do in Summer

by JoAnn Early Macken

LOOK!
BOOKS™

Red Chair Press   Egremont, Massachusetts

Look! Books are produced and published by Red Chair Press:

Red Chair Press LLC   PO Box 333   South Egremont, MA 01258-0333

www.redchairpress.com

 FREE activity page from www.redchairpress.com/free-activities

Publisher's Cataloging-In-Publication Data

Names: Macken, JoAnn Early, 1953-

Title: What we do in summer / by JoAnn Early Macken.

Description: Egremont, Massachusetts : Red Chair Press, [2018] | Series: Look! books : Seasons can be fun | Interest age level: 004-007. | Includes Now You Know fact-boxes, a glossary, and resources for additional reading. | Includes index. | Summary: "Making personal connections to seasonal activity is a powerful way for young readers to learn how each season differs from the others... Do you like to take long walks? Maybe you like digging in a garden or going to the park. Let's discover all the fun things to do in Summer."--Provided by publisher

Identifiers: ISBN 978-1-63440-307-8 (library hardcover) | ISBN 978-1-63440-359-7 (paperback) | ISBN 978-1-63440-311-5 (ebook)

Subjects: LCSH: Summer--Juvenile literature. | Amusements--Juvenile literature. | CYAC: Summer. | Amusements.

Classification: LCC QB637.4 .M332 2018 (print) | LCC QB637.4 (ebook) | DDC 508.2 [E]--dc23

LCCN 2017947527

Photo credits: iStock except for the following; p. 3, 12, 24: Shutterstock; p. 1: Jeff Dinardo; p. 22: Anneli Höglind Thompson

Printed in the United States of America

0718 1P CGF18

Table of Contents

Summer is Warmest

Summer is when the weather is sunny and hot. We take walks and play outside. Grass grows tall. Insects and baby animals hide in the grass. We watch birds visit our feeders.

Green and Growing

Trees grow full and green.
Our garden grows too.
We water plants and
pull out weeds.
We pick pea pods
and berries. Our
vines grow long
and curly.

Tunes in June

A band plays music in the park. We bring a picnic in a basket. We sit on a blanket to eat. Then we play games. Or we may dance to the music. Summer is the time to get active!

JUNE

M	T	W	T	F	S	
	1	2	3	4	5	
7	8	9	10	11	12	
14	15	16	17	18	19	
21	22	23	24	25	26	
28	29	30				

JULY

M	T	W	T	F	S	S
			1	2	3	4
5	6	7	8	9	10	11
12	13	14	15	16	17	18
19	20	21	22	23	24	25
26	27	28	29	30	31	

AUGUST

	T	W	T	F	S	S
						1
3	4	5	6	7	8	
10	11	12	13	14	15	
17	18	19	20	21	22	
24	25	26	27	28	29	

Party On, July

Our street is closed for a block party. All our **neighbors** bring treats to share. We try new foods. We play games with our friends.

Happy Birthday America

We stand in a crowd to watch a parade. We wear red, white, and blue. **Marching** bands play. People clap and cheer. We all wave flags.

13

At night, people fill the park. Fireworks light up the sky. *Boom!* Colors **flash** and colors sparkle.

Good to Know

In the 1730s fireworks shows were popular in England. After America's independence, fireworks were first used to celebrate the special day on July 4, 1777.

We visit the fair. In the barn, huge horses **prance**. A bright light keeps ducklings warm. Farmers show their pigs and cows.

Cooler by the Water

On a hot day, we go to a lake. We hold hands and step in. Tiny fish swim by. When we stand still, they tickle our toes!

Birds look for food on the beach. We look for shells. We build a sand castle. What do you do in summer?

Words to Keep

flash: to shine bright for a short time

marching: walking with regular steps, sometimes to music

neighbor: someone who lives nearby

prance: to walk with high, bouncing steps

vine: a plant that climbs or creeps along the ground

Learn More at the Library

Books (Check out these books to learn more.)

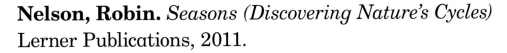

Latta, Sara L. *Why Is It Summer?*
Enslow Publishing, 2012.

Moon, Walter K. *Summer Is Fun!*
(Bumba Books)
Lerner Publications, 2017.

Murray, Julie. *Summer.*
Abdo Kids, 2016.

Nelson, Robin. *Seasons (Discovering Nature's Cycles)*
Lerner Publications, 2011.

Web Sites (Ask an adult to show you these web sites.)

Easy Science for Kids
http://easyscienceforkids.com/all-about-seasons/

University of Illinois: Tree House Weather Kids
https://extension.illinois.edu/treehouse/seasons.cfm?Slide=1

Index

About the Author

JoAnn Early Macken has written more than 130 books for young children. She enjoys taking a canoe down the Wisconsin River in Summer.